Journey of a Humpback Whale

FIRST EDITION
Art Editor Jane Horne; **Senior Art Editor** Cheryl Telfer; **Series Editor** Deborah Lock;
US Editor Adrienne Betz; **DTP Designer** Almudena Diaz; **Production** Shivani Pandey;
Picture Researcher Jo Haddon; **DK Picture Researcher** Sally Hamilton;
Jacket Designer Chris Drew; **Illustrator** Paul Weston; **Indexer** Lynn Bresler;
Reading Consultant Linda Gambrell, PhD;
Whale Consultant William Rossiter, Cetacean Society International

THIS EDITION
Editorial Management by Oriel Square
Produced for DK by WonderLab Group LLC
Jennifer Emmett, Erica Green, Kate Hale, *Founders*

Editors Grace Hill Smith, Libby Romero, Michaela Weglinski;
Photography Editors Kelley Miller, Annette Kiesow, Nicole DiMella; **Managing Editor** Rachel Houghton;
Designers Project Design Company; **Researcher** Michelle Harris; **Copy Editor** Lori Merritt;
Indexer Connie Binder; **Proofreader** Larry Shea; **Reading Specialist** Dr. Jennifer Albro;
Curriculum Specialist Elaine Larson

Published in the United States by DK Publishing
1745 Broadway, 20th Floor, New York, NY 10019

Copyright © 2023 Dorling Kindersley Limited
DK, a Division of Penguin Random House LLC
23 24 25 26 10 9 8 7 6 5 4 3 2 1
001–333913–June/2023

All rights reserved.
Without limiting the rights under the copyright reserved above, no part of this publication may be reproduced, stored in or introduced into a retrieval system, or transmitted, in any form, or by any means (electronic, mechanical, photocopying, recording, or otherwise), without the prior written permission of the copyright owner.
Published in Great Britain by Dorling Kindersley Limited

A catalog record for this book
is available from the Library of Congress.
HC ISBN: 978-0-7440-7224-2
PB ISBN: 978-0-7440-7225-9

DK books are available at special discounts when purchased in bulk for sales promotions, premiums, fundraising, or educational use. For details, contact: DK Publishing Special Markets,
1745 Broadway, 20th Floor, New York, NY 10019
SpecialSales@dk.com

Printed and bound in China

The publisher would like to thank the following for their kind permission to reproduce their images:
a=above; c=center; b=below; l=left; r=right; t=top; b/g=background

Alamy Stock Photo: blickwinkel / S. Meyers 12tc, Hemis.fr / Rieger Bertrand 28-29t; **Dreamstime.com:** John Abramo 1bc, Robert Randall 6, Juergen Schonnop 9cr, Paul Wolf 32crb; **Getty Images:** Moment / Colin Baker 14-15l; **Getty Images / iStock:** lindsay_imagery 3cb; naturepl.com: David Tipling 25tr, Tony Wu 4-5, 10-11

Cover images: *Front:* **Dreamstime.com:** Joni Hanebutt c; **Shutterstock.com:** AQ_taro_neo, Lemberg Vector studio b;
Back: **Shutterstock.com:** AnnstasAg clb, VikiVector cra

All other images © Dorling Kindersley
For more information see: www.dkimages.com

For the curious
www.dk.com

Level 2

Journey of a Humpback Whale

Caryn Jenner

Contents

6 Meeting Triton

16 Finding a Friend

22 Swimming into Danger

26 Coming Home

30 Glossary
31 Index
32 Quiz

Meeting Triton

A humpback whale jumps out of the sea. The whale is named Triton (TRY-tun) after a sea god in ancient myths.

Splash!

Triton has a very powerful tail. The fins at the end of its tail are called "flukes."
Triton has special markings under its flukes.

Every humpback whale has different markings.
Do the flukes of these humpbacks look different to you?

Triton's flukes

Whales live in the sea, but they are not fish. Triton breathes air like humans and other mammals. It can hold its breath underwater for about 30 minutes, but usually it swims to the surface every 4 to 10 minutes.

blowhole

Blowholes

Humpback whales have two blowholes. Hot air shoots out of the blowholes and turns into a mist. Then, the whale breathes in fresh air.

Then Triton breathes through the blowholes at the top of its head. The whale sprays a cloud of mist into the sky!

Sometimes Triton makes special noises under the water.

Triton sings loudly, repeating the same song again and again. The eerie sounds of its song can be heard far away.

Only male humpback whales like Triton sing the special song. Triton sings so other whales will know where to find it, especially female whales.

Triton has spent the winter in the warm water of the Caribbean Sea.
Now Triton is hungry. There isn't much food for a whale here.

Warm Water

In winter, whales swim to warm water to mate and to give birth to their young.

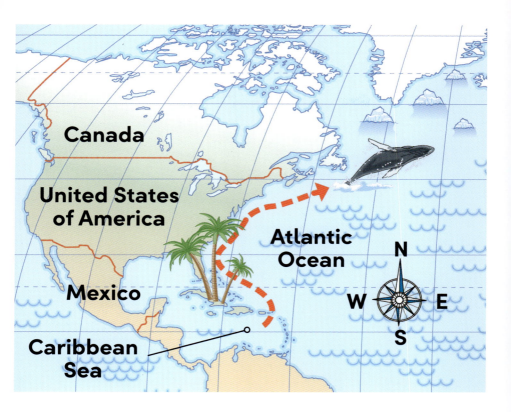

It is time for Triton to swim thousands of miles home to the far north of the Atlantic Ocean. The whale lives there for most of the year. The water is cold in the north, and Triton knows that it will be full of good food to eat.

Swimming

Whales, dolphins, and porpoises move their tails up and down to swim. Fish move their tails from side to side.

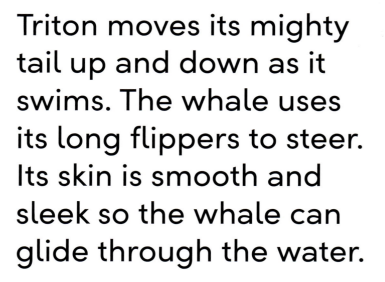

Triton moves its mighty tail up and down as it swims. The whale uses its long flippers to steer. Its skin is smooth and sleek so the whale can glide through the water.

Triton swims at a slow, steady pace. It has a long way to go.

15

Finding a Friend

Triton meets its friend, Spoon, while swimming north.
They travel together for a while, playing as they swim.
Triton and Spoon poke their heads out of the water and look around.

Eyes Underwater

A clear layer of film covers a whale's eyeballs. This protects the whale's eyes from the sting of the salty seawater.

Triton listens carefully. The whale can hear many sounds that help it know what is in the ocean around it.

Now it hears a loud SPLASH! What is that sound?

Splash!

It is Spoon.
It leaps out of the water
in a move called a "breach."
Now it's Triton's turn.
The whale dives backwards
with its flippers high in the air.

Splash!

After all that swimming and playing, Triton and Spoon take a rest.

But Triton is only half asleep. Part of the whale's brain must stay awake to remind it to swim to the surface and take a breath of air.

A mother whale named Salt swims nearby with her calf. This is the calf's first journey north. The calf learns to swim and dive by watching its mother. As it grows, the calf will develop a layer of fat called "blubber," which will give it energy when food is hard to find. Blubber will also keep the calf warm in cold water.

First Breath

Sometimes, a mother whale helps her calf to the surface to take its first breath of air.

Swimming into Danger

Triton dives under the water and swims.
Look out!

It's too late. Triton is caught in a fishing net. The whale must swim to the surface to breathe. It moves its mighty tail.
SWISH!

Finally, Triton finds an opening in the net and swims to the surface. At last, the whale opens its blowholes and breathes the air.

Dangerous Nets

Many whales and dolphins die when they are accidentally caught in nets or other fishing gear.

Food for Whales

Humpback whales feed on small fish such as sardines, herring, and tiny, shrimp-like creatures called "krill."

krill

Triton swims farther north, where the water is colder. The whale takes a giant gulp of cold water. The water is filled with many small fish.

Instead of teeth, Triton has long bristles called "baleen." Triton filters out the extra water through its baleen, then swallows the fish. **Delicious!**

Coming Home

Whales gather wherever there is enough food. Soon Triton sees its friend, Spoon. Together, they dive under the water, blowing bubbles in a big circle to catch a school of herring. Triton surfaces with a mouth full of fish.

Soon, hungry seagulls arrive to see if Triton will share the catch. The whale lets them have a few fish. Triton is almost home, where there will be plenty of food for it and many other whales.

Skreek!

27

At last, Triton arrives home! The journey has taken 35 days. The whale swam nearly 2,000 miles (3,000 kilometers) from the Caribbean Sea to the cold waters off the coast of Canada.

Now Triton will stay here, swimming and playing, and eating as much fish as it wants. Then, when winter comes again, Triton will make the long journey south.

Baleen
Rows of long bristles inside a whale's mouth that are used to strain and collect krill, plankton, and fish from seawater

Blowhole
A nostril on the top of a whale's head that allows it to breathe air

Blubber
A thick layer of fat under a whale's skin that stores energy, keeps the whale warm, and helps it float underwater

Breach
A leaping motion that whales make to lift most of their body out of the water

Caribbean Sea
A large body of water surrounded by Central America, Venezuela, and Colombia that flows into the Atlantic Ocean

Flukes
These are the fins at the end of a whale's tail; all humpback whales have two flukes with unique markings.

Krill
Tiny, shrimp-like creatures that swim near the ocean's surface and make up a major part of a humpback whale's diet

Index

Atlantic Ocean 13

baleen 25

blowholes 9, 22

blubber 20

brain 19

breach 18

breathing 8, 9, 19, 20, 22

bristles 25

bubbles 26

calf 20

Canada 13, 28

Caribbean Sea 12, 13, 28

dolphins 15, 23

eyes 17

filters 25

fins 7

fishing nets 22, 23

flippers 15, 18

flukes 7

head 9, 16

hearing 17

herring 25, 26

krill 25

mammals 8

markings 7

mother whale 20

porpoises 15

Salt 20

sardines 25

seagulls 27

skin 15

sleeping 19

songs and singing 10

sounds 10, 17

Spoon 16, 18, 19, 26

steering 15

swimming 15

tail 7, 15, 22

Triton (sea god) 6

winter 12, 29

Quiz

Answer the questions to see what you have learned. Check your answers in the key below.

1. How long can whales hold their breath underwater?
2. Why do male humpback whales sing?
3. Why does Triton swim thousands of miles home to the Atlantic Ocean?
4. Which direction do whales move their tails to swim?
5. How do humpback whales eat?

1. For about 30 minutes 2. They sing so other whales will know where to find them 3. In order to find food in the cold waters in the north 4. Whales move their tails up and down to swim 5. They take a giant gulp of water and filter their food out through their baleen